# THE BEST OF

# THE BEST OF

## Ice Cream
# A COOKBOOK

Beverly Cox & Malvina C. Kinard

Food Photography by Ellen Silverman

CollinsPublishersSanFrancisco

*A Division of* HarperCollins*Publishers*

First published in USA 1994 by CollinsPublishersSanFrancisco
1160 Battery Street, San Francisco, CA 94111

Produced by Smallwood and Stewart, Inc.,
New York City

© 1994 Smallwood and Stewart, Inc.

Editor: Kathy Kingsley
Food Styling: Mariann Sauvion
Prop Styling: Valorie Fisher

Photography credits: John Margolies: p. 1, 61; Robert Opie: p. 7;
Jean S. Buldain/ Picture Perfect: p. 69; Culver Pictures: p. 40.

Prop credits: Bowls on p. 15 and cup and saucer
on p. 19 from Fishs Eddy; tumbler on p. 39
and glasses on p. 75 from New Glass.

Library of Congress Cataloguing-in-Publication Data

Cox, Beverly
The best of ice cream : a cookbook / Beverly Cox and Malvina C.
Kinard ; food photography by Ellen Silverman
p. cm.
Includes index
ISBN 0-00-255253-1 :
1. Ice cream, ices, etc. I. Kinard, Malvina C. II. Title.
TX795.C69 1993
641.8'62--dc20                                   93-34471
                                                      CIP

Printed in China

# Contents

# Introduction

For many of us, ice cream is as much a passion as a food. It even inspired the mad Roman emperor Nero Claudius Caesar ~ he had snow brought from the Alps by runners, then flavored with fruit juices to produce ices similar to modern sorbets. After the fall of the Roman Empire, flavored ices disappeared from European tables until Marco Polo returned to Italy from Cathay in the late 14th century, bringing similar recipes made with either fruit juice or milk; these had been popular in countries such as China, India, and Persia for centuries.

In the United States, ice cream became a fashionable food in the 18th century. President Washington purchased two newfangled ice cream machines for Mount Vernon, and he ran up an impressive $200 bill for indulging in the delicacy at an ice cream establishment in New York City.

*19th-century advertisement for ice cream machines*

Both Thomas Jefferson and the consummate hostess Dolley (Mrs. James) Madison served "iced creams" at dinners in Philadelphia.

The crank ice cream freezer, an American invention patented in 1848, revolutionized ice cream making. Soon ice cream parlors began to open in cities and towns across the country and became centers of social activity.

Today, the American love affair with ice cream remains as passionate as ever, but now we can savor this glorious food in an almost unprecedented range of forms and flavors. To the sundaes and shakes and ice cream sodas popularized by ice cream parlors we have added crystalline granitas, densely flavored gelatos, and smooth sherbets. Sorbets, the most ancient of ices, suddenly seem the most modern; they may be savory or sweet, and they can be served as palate cleansers between courses as well as at the end of a meal. As we have become more health conscious, the ingredients in all kinds of iced desserts have become lighter. A typical recipe for rich vanilla ice cream sixty years ago contained 16 egg yolks; today it contains 6. Frozen yogurt also has a legion of avid supporters.

In the pages that follow are dozens of dishes that reflect the enormous diversity of ice cream. Here are the very best recipes for iced fruit drinks and savory sorbets, fruit toppings and frozen yogurts, sophisticated party fare and childhood favorites ~ there is something for everyone. This project has made us popular with family and friends, eager tasters every one. We hope that you will enjoy the recipes as much as we all have.

Beverly Cox and Malvina C. Kinard

# French Vanilla Ice Cream

*Vanilla comes from the fruit of an exotic orchid that grows in the jungles of Mexico and Java. One indication of a fine-quality vanilla ice cream is tiny dark flecks, which indicate that the actual vanilla bean was used. If vanilla beans are not available, add 2 teaspoons of pure vanilla extract to the cooled custard base before freezing.*

| | |
|---|---|
| 2 cups whole milk | ¾ cup sugar |
| 1 vanilla bean | ⅛ teaspoon salt |
| 6 large egg yolks | 2 cups heavy cream, chilled |

In a medium saucepan, over medium heat, bring the milk and vanilla bean just to a simmer. Remove the pan from the heat. Remove the vanilla bean from the milk. Using a small sharp knife, split open the bean and scrape the seeds into the milk. Discard the pod.

In the top of a double boiler or a medium stainless steel bowl, whisk the yolks with the sugar and salt for 3 to 4 minutes, or until pale yellow. Gradually whisk in the hot milk. Place the top of the double boiler or the bowl over a pan of simmering (not boiling) water and cook, whisking constantly, for 8 to 10 minutes, or until the custard thickens enough to coat the back of a spoon. Remove the custard from the water and stir in the cream.

Chill the mixture for 30 minutes, then pour into an ice cream maker and freeze according to the manufacturer's directions. For freezing without an ice cream maker, see p. 91. **Makes about 1 quart.**

*Candied Orange-Vanilla Ice Cream:* Prepare the French Vanilla Ice Cream according to the directions. When the ice cream is half frozen, stir in ⅓ cup finely chopped candied orange zest. Complete the freezing process.

*French Vanilla Ice Cream & Melba Sauce, page 68*

*Toffee Crunch Ice Cream:* Prepare the French Vanilla Ice Cream according to the directions. When the ice cream is half frozen, stir in 2 cups chopped almond toffee. Complete the freezing process.

# Chocolate Ice Cream

*Legend attributes the invention of chocolate ice cream to the late emperor Montezuma, who was so fond of* chocolatl, *the sacred chocolate beverage of the Aztecs, that in the heat of summer he reportedly sent runners to nearby mountaintops to bring back snow, over which the drink was poured.*

2 cups whole milk

4 large egg yolks

I cup sugar

⅛ teaspoon salt

3 ounces unsweetened
   chocolate, melted

2 cups heavy cream, chilled

I teaspoon pure vanilla extract

Chocolate Shavings, for
   decoration (optional)

In a medium saucepan, over medium heat, bring the milk just to a simmer. Remove the pan from the heat and set aside.

In the top of a double boiler or a medium stainless steel bowl, whisk the yolks with the sugar and salt for 3 to 4 minutes, or until pale yellow. Gradually whisk in the hot milk. Place the top of the double boiler or the bowl over a pan of simmering (not boiling) water and cook, whisking constantly, for 8 to 10 minutes, or until the custard thickens enough to coat the back of a spoon. Remove the pan from the water and stir in the chocolate until blended. Stir in the cream and vanilla.

Chill the mixture for 30 minutes, then pour into an ice cream maker and freeze according to the manufacturer's directions. For freezing without an ice cream maker, see p. 91. Decorate with Chocolate Shavings, if desired. **Makes about 1 quart.**

NOTE: To make Chocolate Shavings, using a vegetable peeler, shave strips from a block of chocolate. The chocolate block should be soft enough to scrape, but firm enough for the curls to hold their shape.

# Cappuccino Ice Cream

*For ardent coffee lovers, this ice cream is a must. Enjoy it alone or top with the Hazelnut Whipped Cream and serve as "dessert and coffee" in one.*

2 cups whole milk

2 tablespoons instant coffee powder

3 tablespoons hot water

5 large egg yolks

1 cup sugar

⅛ teaspoon salt

2 cups heavy cream, chilled

1 teaspoon pure vanilla extract

Hazelnut Whipped Cream, for decoration (optional)

In a medium saucepan, over medium heat, bring the milk just to a simmer. Remove the pan from the heat and set aside.

In a small bowl, dissolve the coffee in the hot water. Set aside.

In the top of a double boiler or a medium stainless steel bowl, whisk the yolks with the sugar and salt for 3 to 4 minutes, or until pale yellow. Gradually whisk in the hot milk. Place the top of the double boiler or the bowl over a pan of simmering (not boiling) water and cook, whisking constantly, for 8 to 10 minutes, or until the custard thickens enough to coat the back of a spoon. Remove the

custard from the water and stir in the cream, coffee, and vanilla.

Chill the mixture for 30 minutes, then pour into an ice cream maker and freeze according to the manufacturer's directions. For freezing without an ice cream maker, see p. 91. Before serving, decorate with Hazelnut Whipped Cream, if desired. **Makes about 1 quart.**

NOTE: To make Hazelnut Whipped Cream, in a medium bowl, using an electric mixer set at high, beat 1½ cups chilled heavy cream, 2 tablespoons hazelnut-flavored liqueur (Frangelico), and 1 tablespoon sugar until stiff peaks form.

# Dark Chocolate–Almond Ice Cream

*Cocoa and unsweetened chocolate combine to give this ice cream a rich,
deep chocolaty flavor. For a truly decadent treat, top with
Hot Fudge Sauce (p. 71), or try the Double Chocolate–Almond Ice Cream
variation, which includes chopped white chocolate.*

2 teaspoons unsalted butter

½ cup sliced almonds

2 cups whole milk

4 large egg yolks

1 cup sugar

1½ tablespoons unsweetened
  nonalkalized cocoa powder

⅛ teaspoon salt

3 ounces unsweetened
  chocolate, melted

1 teaspoon pure vanilla extract

½ teaspoon pure almond
  extract

1½ cups heavy cream, chilled

In a small skillet, over medium heat, melt the butter. Add the almonds and sauté until just golden. Remove the almonds and dry on paper towels. Set aside.

In a medium saucepan, over medium heat, bring the milk just to a simmer. Remove the pan from the heat and set aside.

In the top of a double boiler or a medium stainless steel bowl, whisk the yolks with the sugar, cocoa, and salt for 3 to 4 minutes, or until thick and creamy.

Gradually whisk in the hot milk. Place the top of the double boiler or the bowl over a pan of simmering (not boiling) water and cook, whisking constantly, for 8 to 10 minutes, or until the custard thickens enough to coat the back of a spoon. Remove the custard from the water and stir in the chocolate until well blended. Stir in the vanilla and almond extract.

Chill the mixture for 30 minutes, then pour into an ice cream maker and freeze

according to the manufacturer's directions.

Meanwhile, in a medium bowl, using an electric mixer set at high, beat the cream until stiff peaks form; chill until ready to use. When the ice cream is half frozen, fold in the whipped cream and almonds. Complete the freezing process. For freezing without an ice cream maker, see p. 91.

**Makes about 1 quart.**

*Double Chocolate–Almond Ice Cream:* Chop 6 ounces white chocolate into small pieces. Prepare the ice cream according to the directions. When the ice cream is half frozen, fold in the whipped cream, almonds, and white chocolate pieces. Complete the freezing process.

# Burnt-Almond Ice Cream

*Sautéing the almonds in a small amount of butter enhances the rich flavor
of this custard-based ice cream. To make a lighter version, reduce the egg yolks to 4
or even 3 and lightly toast the almonds in a 350°F oven for 8 to 10 minutes.*

2 teaspoons unsalted butter

½ cup sliced almonds

2 cups whole milk

5 large egg yolks

¾ cup sugar

⅛ teaspoon salt

2 cups heavy cream, chilled

1 teaspoon pure vanilla extract

½ teaspoon pure almond
  extract

Chocolate-Dipped Almonds,
  for decoration (optional)

In a small skillet, over medium heat, melt the butter. Add the almonds and sauté until just golden. Remove the almonds and dry on paper towels. Set aside.

In a medium saucepan, over medium heat, bring the milk just to a simmer. Remove the pan from the heat and set aside.

In the top of a double boiler or a medium stainless steel bowl, whisk the yolks with the sugar and salt for 3 to 4 minutes, or until pale yellow. Gradually whisk in the hot milk. Place the top of the double boiler or the bowl over a pan of simmering (not boiling) water and cook, whisking constantly, for 8 to 10 minutes, or until the custard thickens enough to coat the back of a spoon. Remove the custard from the water and stir in the cream, vanilla, and almond extract.

Chill the mixture for 30 minutes, then pour into an ice cream maker and freeze according to the manufacturer's directions. When the ice cream is half frozen, stir in the almonds. Complete the freezing process. For freezing without an ice cream maker, see p. 91. **Makes about 1 quart**.

NOTE: To make Chocolate-Dipped Almonds, melt 3 ounces semisweet chocolate in the top of a double boiler or a small stainless steel bowl over a pan of barely simmering (not boiling) water, stirring until smooth. Or microwave the chocolate in a microwave-safe container, uncovered, on medium (50 percent) power for 1 to 2 minutes, stirring once, until the chocolate is shiny. Remove from the microwave and stir until smooth.

Dip 18 to 20 whole blanched almonds into the chocolate so it covers them about halfway. Let any excess chocolate drip back into the container. Place the almonds on a baking sheet lined with waxed paper and chill for 15 minutes, or until the chocolate is set.

# Mocha Chunk Ice Cream

*Adding ingredients such as chocolate chunks or nuts to
ice cream only after it is partially frozen keeps them from sinking to
the bottom and distributes them more evenly throughout the
ice cream. For this recipe, you can either buy a block of semisweet chocolate
and chop it or purchase a 12-ounce bag of chocolate chunks.*

2 cups whole milk

2 tablespoons instant coffee
powder

3 tablespoons hot water

4 large egg yolks

¾ cup sugar

⅛ teaspoon salt

2 cups heavy cream, chilled

1 teaspoon pure vanilla extract

12 ounces semisweet chocolate,
chopped into small pieces

In a medium saucepan, over medium heat, bring the milk just to a simmer. Remove the pan from the heat and set aside.

In a small bowl, dissolve the coffee in the hot water. Set aside.

In the top of a double boiler or a medium stainless steel bowl, whisk the yolks with the sugar and salt for 3 to 4 minutes, or until pale yellow. Gradually whisk in the hot milk. Place the top of the double boiler or the bowl over simmering (not boiling) water and cook, whisking constantly, for 8 to 10 minutes, or until the custard is thick enough to coat the back of a spoon. Remove the custard from the water and stir in the cream, coffee, and vanilla.

Chill the mixture for 30 minutes, then pour into an ice cream maker and freeze according to the manufacturer's directions. When the ice cream is half frozen, stir in the chocolate pieces. Complete the freezing process. For freezing without an ice cream maker, see p. 91. **Makes about 1½ quarts.**

*Mocha Fudge Swirl Ice Cream:* Prepare

18

Hot Fudge Sauce according to the recipe on p. 71. Prepare the Mocha Ice Cream according to the recipe, but omit the chocolate chunks. Spread about 1 inch of the ice cream in the bottom of a 2-quart container. Spread a thin layer of chocolate sauce over the ice cream. Alternate the ice cream and sauce layers until the container is almost full. Using a wooden spoon, stir once or twice to swirl the ice cream. Cover the ice cream and freeze as directed.

# Pralines-and-Cream Ice Cream

*The pralines used in this recipe are of the Creole variety typical of the old French Quarter in New Orleans. Using caramel-flavored ice cream instead of the more traditional vanilla was the novel idea of our friend Peggy Soulie, an inspired Louisiana cook.*

**Peggy's Pecan Pralines:**

½ cup granulated sugar

½ cup packed light brown sugar

¼ cup milk

1 tablespoon unsalted butter

½ cup pecans, coarsely chopped

½ teaspoon pure vanilla extract

**Caramel Syrup:**

½ cup granulated sugar

½ cup boiling water

**Ice Cream:**

2 cups whole milk

3 large egg yolks

½ cup granulated sugar

⅛ teaspoon salt

1½ teaspoons pure vanilla extract

2 cups heavy cream, chilled

Prepare the pralines: Line a baking sheet with parchment or waxed paper.

In a heavy small saucepan, combine both sugars and the milk. Bring the mixture to a boil over medium heat and cook, stirring constantly, until a candy thermometer registers 228°F. Stir in the butter and pecans and cook, without stirring, until the mixture registers 236°F or forms a soft ball when dropped into ice water. Immediately remove the pan from the heat, and remove the candy thermometer.

Add the vanilla and beat with a wooden spoon for about 1 minute, or until the mixture is slightly thickened but still glossy. Working quickly, drop the mixture by tablespoonfuls onto the prepared baking sheet. If the mixture begins to harden while working with it, place the pan over very low heat to soften it. Let the pralines cool completely. **Makes 10 to 12 pralines.**

Prepare the caramel syrup: In a heavy small skillet, over medium-low heat, cook the sugar, swirling the pan, for 15 minutes, or until the sugar melts and turns an amber color. (If using a lighter-weight skillet, watch carefully so the sugar does not burn.) Gradually stir in the boiling water; the caramelized sugar will harden as the water hits it. Cook over medium heat, stirring constantly, until the mixture becomes liquid. (It's all right if a few bits of sugar refuse to melt.) Remove the skillet from the heat. Strain the caramel syrup through a fine sieve set over a small saucepan and keep warm.

Prepare the ice cream: In a medium saucepan, over medium heat, bring the milk just to a simmer. Remove the pan from the heat and set aside.

In the top of a double boiler or a medium stainless steel bowl, whisk the yolks with the sugar and salt for 3 to 4 minutes, or until pale yellow. Gradually whisk in the hot milk. Place the top of the double boiler or the bowl over a pan of simmering (not boiling) water and cook, stirring constantly, for 8 to 10 minutes, or until the custard thickens enough to coat the back of a spoon. Remove the custard from the water and whisk in the warm caramel syrup and the vanilla.

Chill the mixture for 30 minutes, then pour into an ice cream maker and freeze according to the manufacturer's directions.

Meanwhile, finely chop the pralines. In a medium bowl, using an electric mixer set at high, beat the cream until stiff peaks form; chill until ready to use. When the ice cream is half frozen, fold in the whipped cream and praline pieces. Complete the freezing process. For freezing without an ice cream maker, see p. 91. **Makes about 1 quart.**

# Philadelphia Peach Ice Cream

*Philadelphia, the first capital of the United States, was also one of the first places in the New World where ice cream was enjoyed. Such prominent historical figures as George Washington and Thomas Jefferson craved "iced creams" as much as we do today. The ice cream of that period was made by beating heavy cream mixed with sugar and pureed fruits in a metal bowl set over ice. This delicacy had a texture similar to the soft ice creams sold today.*

4 cups peeled, sliced fresh
    peaches (about 6 medium-
    size ripe peaches)
¾ cup sugar
3 tablespoons fresh lemon juice

1 teaspoon pure vanilla extract
½ teaspoon pure almond
    extract
⅛ teaspoon salt
2 cups heavy cream, chilled

In a food processor fitted with the metal blade or a blender, combine the peaches, sugar, lemon juice, vanilla, almond extract, and salt. Process or blend until the mixture is pureed. Transfer the mixture to a medium bowl. Stir in the cream.

Pour the mixture into an ice cream maker and freeze according to the manufacturer's directions. For freezing without an ice cream maker, see p. 91. **Makes about 1 quart.**

*Brandied Peach–Pistachio Sundae:* Peel, pit, and slice 2 medium-size ripe peaches. In a medium bowl, combine the peaches with ¼ cup brandy and 1 tablespoon fresh lemon juice; let stand for 30 minutes. Place a generous scoop of Philadelphia Peach Ice Cream into each of 4 chilled dessert dishes. Spoon the brandied peaches over the ice cream. Top with whipped cream and chopped pistachios. **Serves 4.**

# Philadelphia Strawberry Ice Cream

*Philadelphia-style, or uncooked, ice creams may have a slightly grainier texture than custard-based ice creams because they lack an emulsifier such as egg yolks. Adding fruit, which acts as an emulsifier, to this style of ice cream greatly improves its texture.*

5 cups fresh strawberries, stems removed

¾ cup sugar

3 tablespoons fresh lemon juice

1 teaspoon pure vanilla extract

⅛ teaspoon salt

2 cups heavy cream, chilled

Chop 1 cup of the strawberries and set aside. In a food processor fitted with the metal blade or a blender, combine the remaining strawberries, the sugar, lemon juice, vanilla, and salt. Process or blend until the mixture is pureed. Transfer the mixture to a medium bowl. Stir in the cream.

Pour the mixture into an ice cream maker and freeze according to the manufacturer's directions. When the ice cream is half frozen, stir in the chopped strawberries. Complete the freezing process. For freezing without an ice cream maker, see p. 91. **Makes about 1 quart.**

*Philadelphia Raspberry Ice Cream:* In a food processor fitted with a metal blade or a blender, puree 1 quart of raspberries. Strain the puree through a fine sieve set over a medium bowl to remove the seeds. Add ⅔ cup sugar, 1½ tablespoons fresh lemon juice, 1 teaspoon pure vanilla extract, ½ teaspoon pure almond extract, and ⅛ teaspoon salt and stir until well blended. Stir in 2 cups chilled heavy cream. Freeze as directed.

# Macadamia Nut Ice Cream

*Buttery-rich and slightly sweet, macadamia nuts are a welcome addition
to ice cream. If you can find only salted nuts, rinse and dry them thoroughly.
Hazelnuts or pistachios can be substituted for the macadamia nuts.*

2 cups whole milk

3 large egg yolks

1 cup sugar

1/8 teaspoon salt

2 cups heavy cream, chilled

1 teaspoon pure vanilla extract

1/2 to 3/4 teaspoon ground
cardamom (optional)

1 cup unsalted macadamia nuts,
coarsely chopped

Chopped fresh pineapple, for
decoration (optional)

In a medium saucepan, over medium heat, bring the milk just to a simmer. Remove the pan from the heat and set aside.

In the top of a double boiler or a medium stainless steel bowl, whisk the yolks with the sugar and salt for 3 to 4 minutes, or until pale yellow. Gradually whisk in the hot milk. Place the top of the double boiler or the bowl over a pan of simmering (not boiling) water and cook, stirring constantly, for 8 to 10 minutes, or until the custard thickens enough to coat the back of a spoon. Remove the custard from the water and stir in the cream, vanilla, and cardamom if desired.

Chill the mixture for 30 minutes, then pour into an ice cream maker and freeze according to the manufacturer's directions. When the ice cream is half frozen, stir in the nuts. Complete the freezing process. For freezing without an ice cream maker, see p. 91.

Scoop the ice cream into chilled dessert dishes and decorate with chopped fresh pineapple, if desired. **Makes about 1 quart.**

# Lavender-Honey Ice Cream

*The use of flowers to scent and flavor food is both an ancient and a very modern practice. In India and among Turkish and North African cooks, rose water and orange flower water are familiar ingredients used to flavor rich puddings and refreshing ices. In Europe, during the Middle Ages, flowers were used extensively in the kitchens of nobility. Except in Provence, where orange blossoms and lavender perfume the air and naturally remain part of the regional cuisine, this tradition died out until recently. This ice cream recipe reflects the revived interest in desserts flavored with flowers. Dried lavender blossoms can be purchased at specialty food stores.*

2 cups whole milk

½ cup honey

1 to 1½ teaspoons dried lavender blossoms

4 thin strips each orange and lemon zest

6 large egg yolks

½ cup sugar

⅛ teaspoon salt

2 cups heavy cream, chilled

2 tablespoons fresh lemon juice

1 teaspoon pure vanilla extract

In a medium saucepan, combine the milk, honey, lavender, and zests. Bring the mixture to a simmer over medium heat, stirring to dissolve the honey. Remove the pan from the heat and allow the mixture to steep for 30 minutes. Strain the mixture through a fine sieve set over a medium bowl and set aside.

In the top of double boiler or a medium stainless steel bowl, whisk the yolks with the sugar and salt for 3 to 4 minutes, or until pale yellow. Gradually whisk in the milk mixture. Place the top of the double boiler or the bowl over a pan of simmering (not boiling) water and cook, stirring constantly, for 8 to 10 minutes, or until the custard thickens enough to coat the back of a spoon. Remove the custard from the water and stir in the cream, lemon juice, and vanilla.

Chill the mixture for 30 minutes, then pour into an ice cream maker and freeze according to the manufacturer's directions. For freezing without an ice cream maker, see p. 91. **Makes about 1½ quarts**.

# Florentine Rice Ice Cream

*According to the famous Italian chef and food historian
Giuliano Bugialli, rice ice cream, made with Arborio rice, is all the
rage in Italy. This dessert, which is creamy but slightly crunchy, will
appeal to those who like both ice cream and rice pudding.*

I quart whole milk

²⁄₃ cup sugar

½ cup uncooked Arborio rice

4 thin strips lemon zest

One 3-inch cinnamon stick

Pinch of salt

⅓ cup grappa or dark rum

½ cup chopped dried apricots

4 large egg yolks

I teaspoon pure vanilla extract

2 cups heavy cream, chilled

In a large saucepan, combine 3 cups of the milk, ⅓ cup of the sugar, the rice, lemon zest, cinnamon stick, and salt. Bring to a boil over medium heat, stirring occasionally. Boil gently for about 12 minutes, or until the rice is nearly tender. Remove the pan from the heat and allow the rice to steep in the milk for at least 30 minutes.

Meanwhile, in a small saucepan, over medium-low heat, warm the grappa or rum. Remove the pan from the heat and stir in the apricots. Allow the apricots to soak for at least 30 minutes.

Strain the rice through a sieve set over a 2-cup measure. Add enough of the remaining milk to the rice liquid to measure 1½ cups. Remove and discard the cinnamon stick and lemon zest from the rice, and set the rice aside.

In the top of a double boiler or a medium stainless steel bowl, whisk the egg yolks with the remaining ⅓ cup sugar for 3 to 4 minutes, or until pale yellow. Gradually stir in the milk mixture. Place the top of the double boiler or the bowl over a pan of simmering (not boiling) water and cook, stirring constantly,

for 8 to 10 minutes, or until the custard thickens enough to coat the back of a spoon. Remove the custard from the water and stir in the rice and vanilla.

Chill the mixture for 30 minutes, then pour into an ice cream maker and freeze according to the manufacturer's directions.

Meanwhile, drain the apricots and set aside, discarding the grappa. In a medium bowl, using an electric mixer set at high, beat the cream until stiff peaks form; chill until ready to use. When the ice cream is half frozen, fold in the whipped cream and drained apricots. Complete the freezing process. For freezing without an ice cream maker, see p. 91. **Makes about 1 quart.**

# Crystallized Ginger Ice Cream

*"To ginger" means "to put spirit into," and adding crystallized ginger to ice cream does just that. Preparing your own ice cream will produce the best results, but if time is short, fold chopped crystallized ginger into slightly softened store-bought vanilla ice cream to create a memorable last-minute dessert.*

2 cups whole milk

4 large egg yolks

1 cup sugar

⅛ teaspoon salt

2 cups heavy cream, chilled

1 teaspoon pure vanilla extract

¾ cup chopped crystallized ginger

Thin strips of crystallized ginger, for decoration (optional)

In a medium saucepan, over medium heat, bring the milk just to a simmer. Remove the pan from the heat and set aside.

In the top of a double boiler or a medium stainless steel bowl, whisk the yolks with the sugar and salt for 3 to 4 minutes, or until pale yellow. Gradually whisk in the hot milk. Place the top of the double boiler or the bowl over a pan of simmering (not boiling) water and cook, stirring constantly, for 8 to 10 minutes, or until the custard thickens enough to coat the back of a spoon. Remove the custard from the water and stir in the cream and vanilla.

Chill the mixture for 30 minutes, then pour into an ice cream maker and freeze according to the manufacturer's directions. When the ice cream is half frozen, stir in the chopped ginger. Complete the freezing process. For freezing without an ice cream maker, see p. 91.

Scoop the ice cream into chilled dessert dishes and decorate with strips of crystallized ginger, if desired. **Makes about 1 quart.**

# Japanese Green Tea Ice Cream

*Green tea ice cream reflects the influence of two cultures.
How this dessert came to be served in Japanese restaurants worldwide is
a mystery. It may well be the result of the cross-cultural exchange of
ideas and ingredients over the last 20 years among chefs.*

2 tablespoons green tea leaves
⅓ cup boiling water
2 cups half-and-half
3 large egg yolks
¾ cup sugar

⅛ teaspoon salt
2 cups heavy cream, chilled
1 to 2 drops green food coloring
  (optional)

Place the tea leaves in a small bowl. Pour the boiling water over them and allow to steep for 10 minutes. Strain the tea through a very fine sieve set over a small bowl. Press the leaves to extract as much liquid as possible. Discard the leaves and set the liquid aside.

In a medium saucepan, over medium heat, bring the half-and-half just to a simmer. Remove the pan from the heat and set aside.

In the top of a double boiler or in a medium stainless steel bowl, whisk the yolks with the sugar and salt for 3 to 4 minutes, or until pale yellow. Gradually whisk in the hot half-and-half. Place the top of the double boiler or the bowl over a pan of simmering (not boiling) water, and cook, stirring constantly, for about 8 to 10 minutes, or until the custard thickens enough to coat the back of a spoon. Remove the custard from the water and stir in the cream and tea. Add the green food coloring, if desired.

Chill the mixture for 30 minutes, then pour into an ice cream maker and freeze according to the manufacturer's directions. For freezing without an ice cream maker, see p. 91. **Makes about 1 quart.**

# Banana Ice Cream

*When selecting bananas for ice cream, look for
those with a solid yellow color and no hint of green at the tips.
Store them in a dry, moderately warm place.*

| | |
|---|---|
| 2 cups whole milk | 2 cups heavy cream, chilled |
| 3 large egg yolks | 2 teaspoons pure vanilla extract |
| 1 cup sugar | 2 large ripe bananas |
| ⅛ teaspoon salt | 3 tablespoons fresh lemon juice |

In a medium saucepan, over medium heat, bring the milk just to a simmer. Remove the pan from the heat and set aside.

In the top of a double boiler or a medium stainless steel bowl, whisk the yolks with the sugar and salt for 3 to 4 minutes, or until pale yellow. Gradually whisk in the hot milk. Place the top of the double boiler or the bowl over a pan of simmering (not boiling) water and cook, stirring constantly, for 8 to 10 minutes, or until the custard thickens enough to coat the back of a spoon. Remove the custard from the water and stir in the cream and vanilla.

Chill the mixture for 30 minutes, then pour into an ice cream maker and freeze according to the manufacturer's directions.

Meanwhile, in a small bowl, mash the bananas with the lemon juice. When the ice cream is half frozen, stir in the bananas. Complete the freezing process. For freezing without an ice cream maker, see p. 91. **Makes about 1 quart.**

*Caramel Banana Parfait:* Prepare either of the Caramel Sauces on page 67 and keep warm over low heat. Place one scoop of Banana Ice Cream into each of 6 chilled parfait glasses. Top with 2 tablespoons of the warm sauce, then another scoop of ice cream. Top with more warm sauce and sprinkle with chopped walnuts. **Serves 6.**

# Jamaican Rum-Raisin Ice Cream

*Rum, a spirit distilled from fermented molasses or sugar-cane
juice, is native to the West Indies. For optimum flavor, use a high-quality dark rum.
If you prefer, Cognac or brandy can be substituted for the rum.*

½ cup dark rum
1 cup seedless dark raisins
1 ½ cups whole milk
5 large egg yolks

½ cup packed light brown sugar
⅛ teaspoon salt
2 cups heavy cream, chilled
1 teaspoon pure vanilla extract

In a small saucepan, over medium heat, bring the rum just to a simmer. Remove the pan from the heat and stir in the raisins. Allow the raisins to soak for at least 30 minutes.

In a medium saucepan, over medium heat, bring the milk just to a simmer. Remove the pan from the heat and set aside.

In the top of a double boiler or a medium stainless steel bowl, whisk the yolks with the sugar and salt for 3 to 4 minutes, or until light. Gradually whisk in the hot milk. Using a fine sieve, strain the rum into the custard, and set the raisins aside. Whisk the custard until well blended.

Place the top of the double boiler or the bowl over a pan of simmering (not boiling) water and cook, whisking constantly, for 8 to 10 minutes, or until the custard thickens enough to coat the back of a spoon. Remove the custard from the water. Stir in the cream and vanilla.

Chill the mixture for 30 minutes, then pour into an ice cream maker and freeze according to the manufacturer's directions. When the ice cream is half frozen, stir in the reserved raisins. Complete the freezing process. For freezing without an ice cream maker, see p. 91. **Makes about 1 quart.**

# Crème de Cassis Sorbet

*In France, crème de cassis, a liqueur made from black
currants, is combined with dry white wine to make a popular apéritif called
kir. This sorbet is really a frozen kir, which can be served as a palate
cleanser between courses or as a refreshing light dessert.*

1 ¾ cups cold water

1 ½ cups sugar

1 ½ teaspoons unflavored gelatin

2 cups dry white wine

½ cup crème de cassis

¼ cup fresh lemon juice

Frosted Grapes or Frosted
  Strawberries, for decoration
  (optional)

In a medium saucepan, combine 1 ½ cups of the water and the sugar. Cook over medium heat, stirring occasionally, until the sugar is dissolved. Remove the pan from the heat.

In a small bowl, sprinkle the gelatin over the remaining water and let stand for 1 minute to soften. Add the gelatin to the hot syrup and stir until dissolved. Stir in the wine, crème de cassis, and lemon juice. Transfer the mixture to a large bowl.

Chill the mixture for 30 minutes, then pour into an ice cream maker and freeze according to the manufacturer's directions. For freezing without an ice cream maker, see p. 91.

Spoon the sorbet into chilled dessert dishes or stemmed glasses. Decorate with frosted grapes, if desired. **Makes about 1 quart.**

NOTE: To make Frosted Grapes or Frosted Strawberries, in a small bowl, lightly beat 1 large egg white until frothy. Using a small brush, lightly coat clusters of small red grapes or strawberries with the egg white. Spread ¼ cup granulated sugar on a plate. Coat the fruit with the sugar. Let dry on the sugared surface for 30 minutes, or until the coating is crisp and dry.

# Moorish Orange Sorbet

*At the Gazelle d'Or Hotel in Morocco, orange sorbet is
a house speciality, and it is presented in a most imaginative way. Lids are
cut from the tops of small oranges and the pulp is scooped out. A small
hole is pierced in the bottom of each orange shell and in the center of each lid,
and the lids and shells are frozen while the sorbet is prepared. Then a pipe
cleaner is threaded up through the bottom of each shell and knotted at the base.
The oranges are filled with the sorbet and the pipe cleaner is passed
through the lid. The filled shells are suspended from the branches of small
potted trees, which are then brought to the tables for guests to pick.*

3¼ cups cold water

2½ cups sugar

1 tablespoon grated orange zest

2 teaspoons unflavored gelatin

2 cups fresh orange juice
(about 6 oranges)

2 tablespoons fresh lemon juice

1 teaspoon orange flower water
(optional)

Strips of orange zest, for
decoration (optional)

In a medium saucepan, combine 3 cups of the water, the sugar, and zest. Cook over medium heat, stirring occasionally, until the sugar is dissolved. Remove the pan from the heat and set aside.

In a small bowl, sprinkle the gelatin over the remaining water and let stand for 1 minute to soften. Add the gelatin to the hot syrup and stir until dissolved.

Strain the syrup through a fine sieve set over a large bowl. Stir the orange and lemon juices into the syrup. Stir in the orange flower water, if desired.

Chill the mixture for 30 minutes, then pour into an ice cream maker and freeze according to the manufacturer's directions. For freezing without an ice cream maker, see p. 91.

Spoon the sorbet into chilled dessert or stemmed glasses and decorate with strips of orange zest, if desired. Serve immediately. **Makes about 1 quart.**

*Enthusiastic consumers, New York City, 1920s*

# Italian Raspberry Sorbet

*picture p. 2*

*A base of Italian meringue gives this sorbet its sumptuously smooth texture. Using frozen berries cuts down preparation time and speeds the freezing process. To make Italian Strawberry Sorbet, substitute frozen strawberries for the raspberries.*

**Italian Meringue:**

⅓ cup water

¾ cup sugar

3 large egg whites

**Raspberry Flavoring:**

2 (10-ounce) packages frozen raspberries packed in syrup, slightly thawed

⅓ cup fresh lemon juice

3 to 4 tablespoons raspberry brandy (framboise; optional)

Fresh raspberries, for decoration (optional)

Fresh mint leaves, for decoration (optional)

Prepare the Italian Meringue according to the recipe on p. 80, using the proportions listed above.

In a food processor fitted with the metal blade or a blender, combine the raspberries, lemon juice, and raspberry liqueur, if desired. Process or blend until the mixture is pureed. Transfer the mixture to a large bowl. Using a rubber spatula, gently and thoroughly fold the meringue into the berry mixture.

Transfer the mixture to an ice cream maker and freeze according to the manufacturer's directions. For freezing without an ice cream maker, see p. 91.

Spoon the sorbet into chilled dessert dishes or stemmed glasses and decorate with fresh raspberries and mint leaves, if desired. Serve immediately. **Makes about 1 quart.**

# Lime Sorbet

*To extract the most juice from citrus fruits, soak them in*
*hot water for 30 minutes. Before squeezing, roll the fruit back and forth*
*on a hard surface with the palm of your hand. To make Lemon Sorbet,*
*substitute lemon zest and juice for the lime.*

3¼ cups cold water

3 cups sugar

2 teaspoons finely grated
  lime zest

2 teaspoons unflavored gelatin

1½ cups fresh lime juice
  (about 12 limes)

Lime slices, for decoration
  (optional)

In a medium saucepan, combine 3 cups of the water, the sugar, and lime zest. Cook over medium heat, stirring occasionally, until the sugar is dissolved. Remove the pan from the heat.

In a small bowl, sprinkle the gelatin over the remaining water and let stand for 1 minute to soften. Add the gelatin to the hot syrup and stir until dissolved. Stir in the lime juice. Transfer the mixture to a medium bowl. Chill for 30 minutes, then pour into an ice cream maker and freeze according to the manufacturer's directions. For freezing without an ice cream maker, see p. 91.

Spoon the sorbet into chilled dessert dishes or stemmed glasses and decorate with lime slices, if desired. Serve immediately. **Makes about 1 quart.**

*Lime-Thyme Sorbet:* In a medium saucepan, combine the water, sugar, lime zest, and 5 to 6 sprigs fresh thyme. Cook over medium heat, stirring occasionally, until the sugar is dissolved. Remove the pan from the heat. Add the gelatin mixture and stir until dissolved. Let the mixture stand for 20 minutes, then strain through a sieve set over a medium bowl. Discard the thyme sprigs. Stir in the lime juice and freeze as directed.

# Chocolate Sorbet

*The essence of chocolate shines through in this pure and simple dessert. Serve a single refreshing scoop in a frosty glass or combine scoops of contrasting flavors such as chocolate and Crème de Cassis Sorbet (p. 37) or Italian Raspberry Sorbet (p. 41).*

3½ cups water

1½ cups sugar

4 ounces unsweetened chocolate, coarsely chopped

1 teaspoon pure vanilla extract

Whipped cream, for decoration (optional)

Chocolate Shavings, for decoration (p. 12; optional)

In a medium saucepan, combine the water and sugar. Cook over medium-high heat, stirring occasionally, until the sugar is dissolved. Reduce the heat to medium-low and simmer for 3 to 4 minutes without stirring. Remove the pan from the heat.

Put the chocolate in a food processor fitted with the metal blade and process until finely chopped. With the motor running, pour 1 cup of the hot syrup through the feed tube and process until the chocolate is melted and the mixture is smooth. Whisk the chocolate mixture back into the remaining syrup. Stir in the vanilla.

Chill the mixture for 30 minutes, then pour into an ice cream maker and freeze according to the manufacturer's directions. For freezing without an ice cream maker, see p. 91.

Spoon the sorbet into chilled dessert dishes or stemmed glasses and decorate with whipped cream and Chocolate Shavings, if desired. Serve immediately. **Makes about 1 quart.**

*Mocha Sorbet:* Add 1 tablespoon instant coffee powder to the chocolate before adding the hot syrup. Proceed as directed.

*Chocolate Mint Sorbet:* Add a few drops of mint extract along with the vanilla to the sorbet mixture. Proceed as directed.

# Mocha Gelato

*Gelati, the refreshing ice cream popular in Italy,*
*are easy to make and very satisfying. To make Coffee Gelato, follow the recipe*
*below, substituting unflavored whole milk for the chocolate milk.*

I quart chocolate milk
⅔ cup sugar

¼ cup instant coffee powder
I teaspoon pure vanilla extract

In a medium saucepan, over medium heat, bring the chocolate milk just to a simmer. Remove the pan from the heat.

In a small bowl, combine the sugar and coffee. Gradually stir this mixture into the milk until well blended. Stir in the vanilla. Transfer the mixture to a large bowl.

Chill the mixture for 30 minutes, then pour into an ice cream maker and freeze according to the manufacturer's directions. For freezing without an ice cream maker, see p. 91. **Makes about 1 quart.**

*Mocha Glacé:* In a food processor fitted with the metal blade or a blender, combine 2 cups of the Mocha Gelato and 1 cup cold coffee. Process or blend until slushy. Serve in a tall glass topped with whipped cream, if desired. **Serves 1.**

# Granitas

*Granitas are a sophisticated version of the snow cone.*
*Where sorbets are light and smooth, granitas are icy and crystallized.*
*They are the easiest of frozen desserts to make, requiring*
*neither stirring nor special equipment.*

## Lemon Granita

*picture opposite*

1 ½ cups fresh lemon juice
(about 6 lemons)
3 cups water
1 cup sugar
Thin strips of lemon zest, for
decoration (optional)

In a medium bowl, combine the lemon juice, water, and sugar. Transfer the mixture to a shallow metal baking pan. Freeze for 1½ to 2 hours, or until firm.

To serve, remove the granita from the freezer and scrape with the edge of a spoon to gather up the crystals. Spoon into chilled dessert dishes and decorate with thin strips of lemon zest, if desired. Serve immediately. **Makes 1 quart.**

## Granita di Café

4 cups hot, brewed espresso
1/4 cup sugar
2 tablespoons licorice-flavored liqueur
(anisette; optional)
Whipped cream, for decoration
(optional)

In a medium bowl, combine the coffee, sugar, and liqueur, if desired. Let the mixture cool, then transfer to a shallow metal baking pan. Freeze for 1½ to 2 hours, or until firm.

To serve, remove the granita from the freezer and scrape with the edge of a spoon to gather up the crystals. Spoon into chilled dessert dishes and decorate with whipped cream, if desired. Serve immediately. **Makes 1 quart.**

# Simca's Apricot Ice

*Malvina recorded this unusual recipe during a visit with her friend Simone Beck in the south of France in 1968. It brings back memories of fields of blooming wild flowers, ready for the perfume factories of Grasse. But more vivid is the memory of Simone Beck's fragrant kitchen. Simca, as she was affectionately known, was a well-known author and teacher of French cuisine. She often served this ice to guests on her terrace looking over the flower fields.*

¾ cup granulated sugar
¾ cup packed dark
   brown sugar
2½ cups water
¾ pound dried apricots

3 to 4 strips lemon zest
1 cup dry white wine
½ cup fresh lemon juice
Fresh mint, for decoration
   (optional)

In a medium saucepan, combine both the sugars and the water. Bring the mixture to a boil over medium heat, stirring occasionally until the sugar is dissolved. Add the apricots and lemon zest. Cook over medium-low heat, stirring occasionally, for about 10 minutes, or until the apricots are tender. Remove the pan from the heat and set aside to cool.

Discard all but 1 strip of lemon zest. In a food processor fitted with the metal blade, combine the apricot mixture, wine, and lemon juice and process until pureed. Transfer the mixture to a large bowl.

Chill the mixture for 30 minutes, then pour into an ice cream maker and freeze according to the manufacturer's directions. For freezing without an ice cream maker, see p. 91.

Spoon the ice into chilled dessert dishes or stemmed glasses and decorate with mint leaves, if desired. Serve immediately. **Makes 1 quart.**

# Russian Tomato Ice

*Traditionally, savory ices and sorbets made with wine were served as palate cleansers between rich courses at formal dinners. With today's trend toward fewer courses and lighter eating, savory ices make a very modern appetizer.*

2 teaspoons finely grated lime zest

¼ cup fresh lime juice

4 cups canned tomato juice, chilled

½ cup vodka, chilled

1 tablespoon Worcestershire sauce

2 teaspoons minced onion

1 teaspoon hot pepper sauce

Pinch of salt

Small celery stalks with leaves, for decoration (optional)

Lime or lemon slices or small wedges, for decoration (optional)

In a medium bowl, combine the lime zest and juice, tomato juice, vodka, Worcestershire sauce, onion, hot pepper sauce, and salt. Transfer the mixture to a shallow metal baking pan or to several clean, undivided metal ice cube trays. Freeze the mixture for 1½ to 2 hours, or until firm.

To serve, remove the ice from the freezer and allow it to soften slightly. Spoon it into chilled dessert dishes or stemmed glasses. Decorate with celery stalks and lemon or lime slices, if desired. Serve immediately. **Makes about 1 quart.**

# Strawberry-Rhubarb Sorbet

*When choosing rhubarb, look for firm stalks with a bright, glossy appearance. Store rhubarb in the refrigerator after removing the leaves.*

4 cups diced rhubarb
(about 1 pound stalks)

2¼ cups sugar

1¾ cups cold water

1½ teaspoons unflavored gelatin

1 quart fresh strawberries, stems removed

3 tablespoons fresh lemon juice

Small fresh strawberries, for decoration (optional)

Preheat the oven to 350°F. Put the rhubarb in a shallow baking dish and toss with ¾ cup of the sugar. Cover the dish with foil and bake for 35 to 40 minutes, or until the rhubarb is tender when tested with a fork. Set aside.

In a medium saucepan, combine the remaining 1½ cups sugar and 1½ cups of the water. Cook over medium heat, stirring occasionally, until the sugar is dissolved. Remove the pan from the heat and set aside.

In a small bowl, sprinkle the gelatin over the remaining water and let stand for 1 minute to soften. Add the gelatin to the hot syrup and stir until dissolved. Transfer the mixture to a large bowl.

In a food processor fitted with the metal blade, combine the rhubarb, strawberries, and lemon juice and process until pureed. Add the fruit mixture to the syrup and stir to blend.

Chill the mixture for 30 minutes, then pour into an ice cream maker and freeze according to the manufacturer's directions. For freezing without an ice cream maker, see p. 91.

Spoon the sorbet into chilled dessert dishes or stemmed glasses and decorate with fresh strawberries, if desired. Serve immediately. **Makes about 1 quart.**

# Frozen Yogurt

*Frozen yogurt was originally created for health food enthusiasts as an alternative to ice cream. It has become a mainstream favorite because it's delicious as well as relatively low in fat.*

## Frozen Peach Yogurt

4 cups peeled, sliced fresh
    peaches (about 6 medium-size
    ripe peaches)
¾ cup sugar or ½ cup honey
2 tablespoons fresh lemon juice
1 pint low-fat vanilla yogurt
½ teaspoon pure almond extract

In a food processor fitted with the metal blade, combine the peaches, sugar, and lemon juice and process until pureed. Transfer the mixture to a medium bowl and stir in the yogurt and almond extract. Pour into an ice cream maker and freeze according to the manufacturer's directions. For freezing without an ice cream maker, see page 91. **Makes about 1 quart.**

## Frozen Berry Yogurt

1 quart fresh strawberries, stems
    removed
⅓ cup honey
1 pint plain low-fat yogurt
½ teaspoon pure vanilla extract

In a food processor fitted with the metal blade, combine the strawberries and honey and process until pureed. Transfer the mixture to a medium bowl and stir in the yogurt and vanilla. Pour into an ice cream maker and freeze according to the manufacturer's directions. For freezing without an ice cream maker, see p. 91. **Makes about 1 quart.**

# Frozen Berry Soufflé

*This spectacular dessert is easy to make, and because it uses
frozen raspberries, it can be served year-round. Your noncooking guests might
be puzzled as to how a soufflé that rises above the top of the dish can be frozen.
Don't tell them about the paper collar, and perhaps they won't figure it out.
Strawberries can be substituted for raspberries in this recipe.*

1½ cups half-and-half

3 large egg yolks

½ cup sugar

⅛ teaspoon salt

1 (10-ounce) package frozen
   raspberries packed in syrup,
   thawed

1 teaspoon pure vanilla extract

3 tablespoons raspberry brandy
   (framboise; optional)

2 cups heavy cream, chilled

Whipped cream, for decoration
   (optional)

Fresh raspberries, for decoration
   (optional)

Tie a double thickness of waxed paper around the top of a 1 quart soufflé dish to form a "collar" that extends 2 to 3 inches above the rim of the dish.

In a medium saucepan, over medium heat, bring the half-and-half just to a simmer. Remove the pan from the heat and set aside.

In the top of a double boiler or a medium stainless steel bowl, whisk the yolks with the sugar and salt for 3 to 4 minutes, or until pale yellow. Gradually whisk in the hot half-and-half. Place the top of a double boiler or the bowl over a pan of simmering (not boiling) water and cook, stirring constantly, for 8 to 10 minutes, or until the custard thickens enough to coat the back of a spoon. Chill the custard for 30 minutes.

Press the raspberries, with their syrup, through a fine sieve set over a small bowl. Discard the seeds. Stir the raspberry puree and vanilla, along with the liqueur if desired, into the custard.

In a medium bowl, using an electric mixer set at high, beat the cream until stiff peaks form. Using a rubber spatula, gently and thoroughly fold the cream into the custard. Pour the mixture into the prepared soufflé dish and freeze for at least 3 hours, or until firm.

To serve, remove the collar from the soufflé dish. Let the soufflé stand at room temperature for 15 minutes to soften slightly. Decorate with whipped cream and fresh raspberries, if desired. **Serves 6 to 8.**

# Baked Alaska

*Baked Alaska has always been a showstopper, but the time ~
and timing ~ required to make it often discourage all but the most inspired
cooks. In this recipe, the traditional last-minute unmolding of
the ice cream onto a layer of cake is avoided by filling a hollowed-out pound
cake with softened ice cream and freezing it. The assembled
dessert can be made up to 2 weeks in advance and frozen. Before serving,
all that's required is 5 minutes in the oven.*

1 (10½-ounce) prepared all-butter pound cake

½ brandied pear, chopped (see Note)

1 pint French Vanilla Ice Cream (p. 10) or store-bought vanilla ice cream, slightly softened

¼ cup brandied pear syrup (see Note)

1 teaspoon Poire William (pear eau de vie; optional)

1 recipe Italian Meringue (p. 80)

Confectioners' sugar, for dusting (optional)

Using a serrated knife, cut a ½-inch-thick lid off the top of the pound cake. Set aside. Cut around the inner perimeter of the cake to form a shell ½ inch thick, and, using a small sharp knife or a spoon, hollow out the cake. Place the cake and the lid in the freezer until ready to fill.

In a medium bowl, fold the chopped pear into the softened ice cream.

In a small bowl, combine the pear syrup and Poire William. Brush the inside of the cake shell with the mixture.

Fill the cake shell with the ice cream mixture, smoothing the top with a spoon. Place the cake lid on top. Wrap the cake in plastic or foil and freeze for at least 1 hour, or until completely frozen.

Preheat the oven to 475°F. Prepare the Italian Meringue according to the recipe. Place the frozen cake on a cool ovenproof metal serving platter or a double thickness of lightly oiled heavy-duty aluminum

foil. Using a small spatula, quickly frost the cake with a $\frac{1}{2}$-inch-thick layer of Italian Meringue. Fill a large pastry bag fitted with a No. 6 star tip with the remaining meringue and decorate as desired.

Lightly sprinkle the Baked Alaska with confectioner's sugar, if desired. Bake for 5 minutes, or until the meringue is lightly browned. **Serves 6 to 8.**

NOTE: To prepare brandied pears; in a medium saucepan, combine 1 cup sugar and $1\frac{1}{2}$ cups water. Bring the syrup to a boil, stirring until the sugar dissolves. Reduce the heat to low and simmer for 10 minutes without stirring. While the syrup is cooking, peel, halve, and core 2 ripe but firm pears.

Add the pears to the syrup and simmer until tender, about 5 minutes. Remove the pan from the heat. Add 1 tablespoon Cognac to the syrup. Allow the pears to cool in the syrup.

NOTE: To prepare ahead of time, cover the filled cake with the meringue, then freeze to firm it slightly. Insert 2 or 3 wooden skewers into the cake. Cover loosely but securely with a double thickness of foil and freeze.

# Amaretti Tortoni

*This frozen mousse is a well-loved Italian dessert.*
*Make it as suggested here with Marsala or sherry, or try it with*
*a tablespoon of rum or cherry liqueur.*

1 cup crushed amaretti cookies
  or macaroons

1½ cups light cream

3 to 4 tablespoons Marsala or
  cream sherry (optional)

1 teaspoon pure vanilla extract

⅓ cup sifted confectioners'
  sugar

Pinch of salt

2 cups heavy cream, chilled

Amaretti cookies, for decoration
  (optional)

½ cup sliced almonds, lightly
  toasted, for decoration
  (optional)

Chill six 6-ounce metal molds until ready to use.

In a large bowl, combine the amaretti crumbs, light cream, Marsala, if desired, and vanilla. Chill the mixture for 1 hour. Stir in the sugar and salt until well blended.

In a medium bowl, using an electric mixer set at high, beat the heavy cream until stiff peaks form. Using a rubber spatula, gently and thoroughly fold the whipped cream into the amaretti mixture.

Spoon the mixture into the chilled molds, filling them to the top. Gently tap the molds on a work surface to remove any air bubbles. Freeze the tortoni for 3 hours, or until firm.

To unmold, briefly dip the molds in hot water, then invert onto chilled dessert plates and remove the molds. Decorate with amaretti cookies and toasted almonds, if desired. Serve immediately. **Serves 6.**

NOTE: The Amaretti Tortoni can also be made in 8 paper-lined muffin cups or six 6-ounce soufflé cups.

# Frozen Chocolate-Banana Pie

*Ice cream pies are festive and easy to make.*
*If there isn't time to prepare your own ice cream, simply allow 1 quart of*
*store-bought French vanilla ice cream to soften slightly, then fold in 2 mashed*
*bananas along with 3 tablespoons of fresh lemon juice.*

**Chocolate Cookie Crust:**

Approximately 30 plain
   chocolate cookie wafers
6 tablespoons unsalted butter,
   melted

1 recipe Banana Ice Cream
   (p. 35)
Whipped cream, for decoration
   (optional)
Chocolate Curls, for decoration
   (optional)

Prepare the crust: Preheat the oven to 325°F. In a food processor fitted with the metal blade, process the cookies until finely ground. Or, using a rolling pin, crush the wafers between 2 pieces of waxed paper to make fine crumbs. You should have 1 1/2 cups crumbs.

In a small bowl, combine the crumbs and melted butter; stir until well blended. Using the palm of your hand, press the moistened crumbs into the bottom and up the sides of an ungreased 9-inch pie plate. Bake in the center of the oven for 12 to 15 minutes, or until the crust is set.

Put the pie crust on a wire rack to cool. Then chill until ready to fill.

Make the Banana Ice Cream according to the recipe. Spoon the ice cream into the prepared pie crust. Freeze for at least 1 hour, or until firm. Just before serving, decorate the pie with rosettes of whipped cream and Chocolate Curls, if desired. **Serves 8 to 10.**

NOTE: To make Chocolate Curls, melt 4 to 6 ounces of semisweet, bittersweet, milk, or white chocolate. Spread the chocolate thinly on a marble slab or on the back of a baking sheet. If using mar-

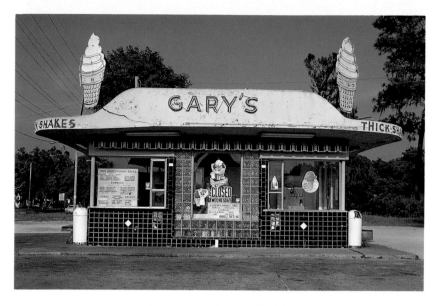

*Ice cream stand, Florida*

ble, let the chocolate cool until set; if using a baking sheet, chill for 5 to 10 minutes, or until set but not brittle. Using a metal spatula held at a 45° angle, scrape the chocolate from the surface to form curls. To prevent melting, handle the curls with a wooden skewer and chill until ready to use.

*Frozen Mocha Pie:* Fill the chilled chocolate crust with Cappuccino Ice Cream, p. 13. Decorate with whipped cream rosettes and chocolate-covered coffee beans, if desired.

*Double Ginger Ice Cream Pie*: Prepare a crumb crust by combining 1 ½ cups gingersnap crumbs with 6 tablespoons melted unsalted butter as directed in the recipe. Fill the chilled baked crust with Crystallized Ginger Ice Cream, p. 33. Decorate with whipped cream rosettes and thin strips of crystallized ginger, if desired.

# Peach-Curaçao Cream

*Frozen creams and mousses are early versions of ice cream that
predate the invention of the mechanical ice cream machine in the late 1700s.
These frozen desserts owe their light texture to the addition of whipped cream;
they are often used as the center of bombes.*

4 cups peeled, sliced fresh
 peaches (about 6
 medium-size ripe peaches)

1 1/4 cups sugar

1/4 cup fresh lemon juice

2 teaspoons unflavored gelatin

1/2 cup Curaçao or other
 orange-flavored liqueur

1/2 cup light cream

1 teaspoon pure vanilla extract

1/2 teaspoon pure almond
 extract

2 cups heavy cream, chilled

Fresh raspberries, for decoration
 (optional)

In a food processor fitted with the metal blade or a blender, combine the peaches, sugar, and lemon juice. Process or blend until the mixture is pureed. Set aside.

In a medium stainless steel bowl, sprinkle the gelatin over the liqueur and let stand for 1 minute to soften.

In a small saucepan, over medium heat, bring the light cream just to a simmer. Pour the cream over the gelatin mixture and stir until the gelatin is dissolved. Add the peach puree and stir until blended. Stir in the vanilla and almond extract.

In a medium bowl, using an electric mixer set at high, beat the heavy cream until stiff peaks form. Using a rubber spatula, gently and thoroughly fold the cream into the peach mixture. Cover the bowl with plastic wrap and freeze for at least 3 hours, or until the cream is firm.

To serve, allow the cream to soften slightly, then spoon it into chilled dessert dishes. Decorate with fresh raspberries, if desired. **Makes about 1 quart.**

# Bombe Othello

*Bombes always announce a special occasion. They are
easy to assemble and can be made in many flavor combinations. Two or more
frozen mixtures, such as an ice cream and mousse, are layered in a round
or oval metal mold, then returned to the freezer for firming up.*

1 recipe Chocolate Ice Cream
   (p. 12)
1 recipe Pistachio-Almond
  Mousse (p. 66)

Toasted sliced almonds,
   for decoration (optional)

Prepare the Chocolate Ice Cream and Pistachio Mousse according to the recipes.

Chill a 2- to 2½-quart metal mold or bowl. Remove the ice cream from the freezer and let stand for 10 minutes to soften slightly. Working quickly with a flexible spatula, spread the ice cream evenly over the inside of the mold to about a ¾-inch thickness. Place the mold in the freezer for 30 minutes, or until the ice cream is firm.

Remove the mold from the freezer and fill it with the mousse, packing it firmly into the cavity. Cover the mold with waxed paper and return it to the freezer for at least 2 hours, or until firm.

To unmold, remove the waxed paper and invert the mold onto a chilled serving platter. Soak a clean towel in hot water, then squeeze out the water. Press the towel over the surface of the mold for 1 to 2 minutes, then gently lift the mold off the frozen dessert. Decorate with toasted sliced almonds, if desired. To serve, dip a knife in hot water, wipe it dry, and slice the bombe into wedges. Serve immediately. **Serves 6.**

# Bombe Cardinal

*Where desserts and sweets are concerned, the term "cardinal,"
referring to the red color of a cardinal's robe, usually applies to a
confection containing strawberries or raspberries.*

1 recipe Philadelphia Strawberry
   Ice Cream (p. 24)

1 recipe Peach-Curaçao Cream
   (p. 62)

Frosted Strawberries, for
   decoration (p. 37; optional)

Prepare the Philadelphia Strawberry Ice Cream and Peach-Curaçao Cream according to the recipes.

Chill a 2- to $2\frac{1}{2}$-quart metal mold or bowl. Remove the ice cream from the freezer and let stand for 10 minutes to soften slightly. Working quickly, with a flexible spatula, spread the ice cream evenly over the inside of the mold to about a $\frac{3}{4}$-inch thickness. Place the mold in the freezer for 30 minutes, or until the ice cream is firm.

Remove the mold from the freezer and fill it with the cream, packing it firmly into the cavity. Cover the mold with waxed paper and return it to the freezer for at least 2 hours, or until firm.

To unmold, remove the waxed paper and invert the mold onto a chilled serving platter. Soak a clean towel in hot water, then squeeze out the water. Press the towel over the surface of the mold for 1 to 2 minutes, then gently lift the mold off the frozen dessert. Decorate the serving platter with Frosted Strawberries, if desired. To serve, dip a knife in hot water, wipe it dry, and slice the bombe into wedges. Serve immediately. **Serves 6.**

# Pistachio-Almond Mousse

*When preparing pistachio nuts it is sometimes difficult
to remove their brown inner skins. To remove this skin, place the pistachios in a
bowl and cover with boiling water. Allow them to stand for 3 minutes, then drain
and rub off the softened skins. Set the nuts on paper towels to dry.*

1 teaspoon unsalted butter

¼ cup sliced almonds

¼ cup shelled, skinned pistachio
nuts, coarsely chopped

2 cups heavy cream, chilled

⅓ cup honey

1 teaspoon pure vanilla extract

½ teaspoon pure almond
extract

3 drops green food coloring
(optional)

1 drop yellow food coloring
(optional)

Pinch of salt

In a small skillet, over medium-low heat, melt the butter. Add the almonds and sauté until just golden. Stir in the pistachios. Remove the nuts and drain on paper towels. Set aside.

In a medium stainless steel bowl, using an electric mixer set at high, beat the cream until soft peaks form. Add the honey, vanilla, almond extract, food coloring, if desired, and salt; beat at high speed until stiff peaks form.

Using a rubber spatula, gently and thoroughly fold the nuts into the whipped cream mixture. Cover the bowl with plastic wrap and freeze for at least 3 hours, or until the mousse is firm.

To serve, allow the cream to soften slightly, then spoon it into chilled dessert dishes. **Makes about 1 quart.**

# Classic Caramel Sauce

*When sugar is heated slowly,
it melts into a syrup, then begins to turn
a golden amber ~ a process called
caramelization, which imparts a deep,
rich flavor to the sugar. To prevent
burning, be sure to use a heavy-bottomed
saucepan when making this sauce.*

¾ cup sugar
¼ cup light corn syrup
½ cup heavy cream
½ teaspoon pure vanilla extract
Pinch of salt

In a heavy medium-size saucepan, combine the sugar and corn syrup. Cook over medium-low heat, stirring occasionally, for 12 to 15 minutes, or until the sugar is completely melted and the mixture turns a light golden brown. Remove the pan from the heat and carefully stir in the cream, vanilla, and salt. Serve the sauce warm. **Makes about 1 cup.**

# Quick Caramel Sauce

*This sauce is sinfully rich and
it couldn't be easier to make. Serve it
warm over vanilla ice cream, then
top with whipped cream and lightly
toasted pecan halves. For a variation,
use chocolate-flavored caramels.*

½ pound vanilla caramel candies
1 cup heavy cream

Combine the caramels and cream in the top of a double boiler or a small stainless steel bowl set over a pan of simmering (not boiling) water, stirring until the caramels are melted and the mixture is smooth. Remove the sauce from the water. Serve the sauce warm. **Makes about 1½ cups.**

# Melba Sauce

*picture p. 11*

*This sauce is often served as part of Coupe Melba,
a dessert created in the late 1800s by Auguste Escoffier to honor Nellie Melba,
an Australian diva. Coupe Melba is a combination of poached peaches,
vanilla ice cream, and Melba Sauce presented in chilled stemmed dessert glasses,
or coupes. The dessert can also be made with poached pears.*

1 (10-ounce) package frozen raspberries packed in syrup, thawed

¼ cup sugar
1 tablespoon fresh lemon juice

Press the raspberries through a fine sieve set over a medium bowl to remove the seeds. Discard the seeds. Transfer the raspberries to a small saucepan. Stir in the sugar and cook over medium heat, stirring frequently, for 3 to 5 minutes, or until the sauce starts to thicken. Remove the pan from the heat. Stir in the lemon juice until well blended. Serve warm or at room temperature. **Makes ¾ cup.**

*Coupe Melba:* In a medium saucepan, bring 1½ cups water and 1 cup sugar to a boil over medium-high heat. Add 4 peeled and pitted fresh peach halves to the syrup. Cook, covered, over low heat for 10 to 12 minutes, or until softened. Remove the pan from the heat. Stir in 2 teaspoons pure vanilla extract. Cool the peaches in the syrup.

Place 1 peach half in each of 4 chilled coupes or stemmed glasses. Top each half with a generous scoop of French Vanilla Ice Cream, p. 10. Drizzle with the Melba Sauce. Serve immediately. **Serves 4.**

*Ice cream sign, Provence*

# Crème Anglaise

*Classic crème Anglaise is one of the most versatile
dessert sauces. To vary the flavor, reduce the vanilla extract to 1 teaspoon and
add 1 tablespoon of rum, Cognac, brandy, or orange-flavored liqueur.
Other variations include adding 1 tablespoon of instant coffee powder or 2 ounces
of semisweet chocolate with the hot milk.*

1¾ cups whole milk
4 large egg yolks

½ cup sugar
2 teaspoons pure vanilla extract

In a medium saucepan, over medium heat, bring the milk just to a simmer. Remove the pan from the heat and set aside.

In the top of a double boiler or a medium stainless steel bowl, whisk the yolks with the sugar for 3 to 4 minutes, or until pale yellow. Gradually whisk in the hot milk. Place the top of the double boiler or the bowl over a pan of simmering (not boiling) water and cook, stirring constantly, for 8 to 10 minutes, or until the custard thickens enough to coat the back of a spoon. Remove the sauce from the water and stir in the vanilla. Serve the sauce warm or chilled. **Makes about 2 cups.**

# Hot Fudge Sauce

*This classic sauce is delicious over ice cream.*
*If you cook it 3 to 4 minutes longer, it will harden like the chocolate*
*sauces used to dip soft ice cream cones.*

2 ounces unsweetened
  chocolate, coarsely chopped
1 tablespoon unsalted butter
⅓ cup boiling water
1 cup sugar

2 tablespoons unsweetened
  cocoa powder
2 tablespoons light corn syrup
Pinch of salt
1 teaspoon pure vanilla extract

In a heavy medium-size saucepan, combine the chocolate and butter. Cook over very low heat, stirring constantly, until the chocolate is melted and the mixture is smooth. Slowly stir in the boiling water. Add the sugar, cocoa, corn syrup, and salt and stir until well blended.

Cook over medium heat, stirring frequently, until the sauce comes to a gentle boil. Boil over medium-low heat, without stirring, for 5 minutes. Remove the pan from the heat and stir in the vanilla. Serve immediately.

To reheat leftover sauce, place the sauce in the top of a double boiler or a small stainless steel bowl set over a pan of simmering (not boiling) water and cook, stirring frequently, for 2 to 3 minutes, or until heated through. Or microwave the sauce in a small microwave-safe container, covered loosely with waxed paper, on medium (50 percent) power for 1 to 2 minutes, stirring once, until heated through. **Makes about 1½ cups.**

*Spirited Fudge Sauce:* Add 1 tablespoon whiskey, rum, or orange-flavored liqueur just before serving.

# Mocha Sauce

*Originally the term "mocha" or "moka" referred to a fragrant variety of coffee bean grown in Mocha, Arabia. Over the years, it has come to be associated with a mixture of coffee and chocolate, as in this sauce.*

2 ounces unsweetened chocolate, coarsely chopped
2 tablespoons unsalted butter
1/3 cup boiling water
1 cup sugar

3 tablespoons light corn syrup
3 to 4 teaspoons instant coffee powder
1 teaspoon pure vanilla extract

In a heavy medium-size saucepan, combine the chocolate and butter. Cook over very low heat, stirring constantly, until the chocolate is melted and the mixture is smooth. Slowly stir in the boiling water. Add the sugar, corn syrup, and coffee and stir until well blended.

Bring the mixture to a simmer over medium-low heat and cook, stirring constantly, for 3 to 5 minutes, or until the sauce begins to thicken. Remove the pan from the heat. Stir in the vanilla. Serve the sauce warm or at room temperature.

To reheat, place the sauce in the top of a double boiler or a small stainless steel bowl set over a pan of simmering (not boiling) water and cook, stirring frequently, for 2 to 3 minutes, or until heated through. Or microwave the sauce in a small microwave-safe container, covered loosely with waxed paper, on medium (50 percent) power for 1 to 2 minutes, stirring once, until heated through. **Makes about 1 1/4 cups.**

# Fruit Coulis

*Fruit coulis are the simplest and freshest of dessert sauces.*
*They are made from pureed fresh fruit and lemon or lime juice sweetened with*
*sugar. A variety of berries and fruits may be used to make coulis;*
*strawberries, raspberries, blackberries, kiwifruit, mangoes, and papayas*
*are all good candidates. When making a sauce of raspberries*
*or other berries with small seeds, you can remove the seeds by pressing*
*the puree through a strainer or fine sieve.*

## Strawberry Coulis

1 pint fresh strawberries, stems removed
1 to 2 tablespoons fresh lemon juice
2 to 3 tablespoons superfine sugar

In a food processor fitted with the metal blade or a blender, combine the strawberries and lemon juice and process or blend until pureed. Transfer the mixture to a small bowl and stir in the sugar to taste. **Makes about 1 cup.**

## Kiwifruit Coulis

6 ripe kiwifruit
1 to 2 tablespoons fresh lemon juice
2 to 3 tablespoons superfine sugar

Peel the kiwifruit. In a food processor fitted with the metal blade or a blender, combine the kiwifruit and lemon juice and process or blend until pureed. Transfer the mixture to a small bowl and stir in the sugar to taste. **Makes about 1 cup.**

# Cherries Jubilee

*This classic restaurant dessert is as simple to prepare
as it is showy, and it makes an elegant ending to any dinner. Ideally,
the cherries should be flamed at the table in a chafing dish and
spooned over the ice cream while still burning (see Note).
Apricot or peach halves in heavy syrup can be substituted for the
cherries and served in the same manner.*

1 (16½-ounce) can pitted dark
    sweet Bing cherries in heavy
    syrup
1 tablespoon cornstarch
2 tablespoons Cognac, brandy,
    or rum

1 tablespoon orange-flavored
    liqueur (Cointreau)
1 recipe French Vanilla Ice
    Cream (p. 10)

Reserve ¼ cup of the cherry syrup. Pour the cherries with the remaining syrup into a large skillet.

In a small bowl, dissolve the cornstarch in the reserved syrup. Add this mixture to the cherries, stirring until well blended.

Bring the cherry mixture to a simmer over medium heat, stirring frequently. Simmer for 1 to 2 minutes, or until the sauce thickens slightly. Remove the skillet from the heat. Stir in the Cognac and liqueur.

To serve, place a generous scoop of French Vanilla Ice Cream into each of 6 dessert dishes. Spoon the warm cherries and syrup over the ice cream. Serve immediately. **Serves 6.**

NOTE: To serve Cherries Jubilee flamed, cook the cherries as directed and remove the pan from the heat. In a small saucepan, over low heat, warm ½ cup of Cognac, brandy or rum and ¼ cup orange-flavored liqueur. Remove the pan from the heat. Stir the warm liqueur into the cherries and light, using a long fireplace match. Spoon the flaming cherries and syrup over the ice cream. Serve immediately.

# Butterscotch Sauce

*The flavor of this old-fashioned topping is a blend
of butter and sugar. Spoon it over your favorite ice cream or pound cake.
For an extra taste sensation, try adding toasted, chopped pecans to the sauce
(see the recipe for Butterscotch-Pecan Sauce below).*

½ cup light corn syrup
¾ cup packed dark brown sugar
2 tablespoons unsalted butter

½ cup heavy cream
Pinch of salt
1 teaspoon pure vanilla extract

In a heavy medium-size saucepan, combine the corn syrup, sugar, and butter. Cook over medium heat, stirring frequently, for 4 to 5 minutes, or until the sugar is dissolved. Stir in the cream and salt and cook, stirring frequently, for 3 to 4 minutes, or until slightly thickened. Remove the pan from the heat. Stir in the vanilla and allow the mixture to cool slightly before serving.

To reheat, place the sauce in the top of a double boiler or a medium stainless steel bowl set over a pan of simmering (not boiling) water and cook, stirring frequently, for 2 to 3 minutes, or until heated through. Or microwave the sauce in a small microwave-safe container, covered loosely with waxed paper, on medium (50 percent) power for 1 to 2 minutes, stirring once, until heated through. **Makes about 1½ cups.**

*Butterscotch-Pecan Sauce:* In a small skillet, melt 2 tablespoons unsalted butter over medium heat. Add ½ cup chopped pecans and sauté until golden brown and fragrant. Remove the pan from the heat. Prepare the Butterscotch Sauce as directed, stirring in the pecans along with the vanilla.

# Ice Cream Cones

*It is said that, like many great inventions, ice cream cones were discovered by accident. At the 1904 World's Fair, waffles were being made by hawkers on the street and ice cream was for sale along the way. At one stand they ran out of ice cream containers, so an inventive salesman twisted a thick waffle into a cone shape and filled it with ice cream!*

¾ cup confectioners' sugar

½ cup all-purpose flour

Pinch of salt

2 large egg whites

¼ cup (½ stick) unsalted butter, melted and cooled

¼ teaspoon pure vanilla extract

Pizzelle iron

3 medium-size metal cone-shaped forms or cardboard cones covered with aluminum foil, light oiled

In a medium bowl, sift together the confectioners' sugar, flour, and salt.

In a medium bowl, using an electric mixer set at high, beat the egg whites until stiff peaks form. Using a rubber spatula, gently and thoroughly fold in the sugar mixture. Gently stir in the cooled melted butter and the vanilla.

Bake the batter in a preheated pizzelle iron according to the manufacturer's directions. Using a metal spatula or pancake turner, lift each hot pizzelle from the iron and mold it around a metal form to make a cone. When cool, remove the form from the cone. **Makes 8 to 10 large cones.**

Note: Cooled cones can be stored in an airtight container at room temperature for up to 1 week.

*Dipped Cones:* Melt 4 to 6 ounces semisweet chocolate, and transfer to a small bowl. Dip the top inch of each cone into the chocolate, then roll in colored sprinkles or chopped nuts to cover. Put the cones on a plate and chill for 15 minutes, or until the chocolate is set.

# Ice Cream Cups

*Cookie bowls date back to the Victorian era,
when elaborate food presentations were the rule. Today, the concept
of a cookie bowl for ice cream remains appealing and intriguing. These cookies
are not difficult to make. The only crucial factor is timing: They must be
molded while still warm. Before you start, have everything ready,
and clear enough space to set down a hot baking sheet.*

¼ cup (½ stick) unsalted
    butter, softened
½ cup sugar
2 large egg whites, lightly beaten

½ teaspoon pure vanilla extract
Pinch of salt
½ cup all-purpose flour

Preheat the oven to 350°F. Invert six 6-ounce custard cups on a work surface and lightly grease the bottoms and sides. Line 2 baking sheets with parchment paper. Using a pencil, trace three 6-inch circles onto each sheet of parchment.

In a large bowl, using an electric mixer set at high, cream the butter and sugar until light and fluffy. Beat in the egg whites, vanilla, and salt until well blended. Gently stir in the flour.

Anchor the parchment paper to the baking sheets by putting a small dab of batter under each corner. Using a rubber spatula, spread a thin layer of the batter inside the circles on 1 sheet of parchment. Bake the cookies for 5 to 7 minutes, or until golden brown. Remove the baking sheet from the oven and, while the cookies are still hot, quickly but carefully slide a metal spatula under each cookie and mold it over an inverted cup. Repeat with the remaining batter. When cool, gently remove the cookies from the cups and invert. **Makes 6 cups.**

NOTE: The cooled cookie cups can be stored in an airtight container at room temperature for up to 3 days.

# Italian Meringue

*Italian, or hot syrup, meringue is a versatile and durable member of the meringue family. It may be piped and baked into shells, spread over Baked Alaska (p. 56), or folded into a sherbet, frozen mousse, or soufflé mixture. Unlike hard or soft meringues, which are uncooked, this meringue will not weep, crack, or shrink.*

1 cup sugar
⅓ cup water
3 large egg whites,
    at room temperature

⅛ teaspoon cream of tartar
Pinch of salt
¼ teaspoon pure vanilla extract

In a small saucepan, combine the sugar and water. Swirl the saucepan slowly by the handle over medium-high heat until the sugar dissolves and the mixture comes to a boil; do not stir. Continue to swirl the pan until the syrup becomes clear. Cover the pan and reduce the heat to low.

In a large bowl, using an electric mixer set at medium-low, beat the egg whites for about 1 minute, or until foamy. Add the cream of tartar and salt, increase the mixer speed to high, and beat until stiff peaks form.

Remove the cover from the saucepan and boil the syrup rapidly over medium heat for 1 to 2 minutes, or until the bubbles begin to thicken and a few drops of the hot syrup forms a soft ball when dropped in ice water (238°F on a candy thermometer). Immediately remove the pan from the heat.

Reduce the mixer speed to medium and gradually beat the hot syrup into the egg whites in a slow, steady stream. Add the vanilla and beat on high speed for 6 to 8 minutes, or until the mixture is completely cool. The meringue should be smooth and shiny and hold stiff peaks. Use immediately. **Makes about 3 cups.**

# Individual Meringue Shells

*These individual shells form the base for a meringue glacé,
a classic and always elegant dessert. The shells can be prepared up to
a week ahead, and then the dessert can be assembled at the last minute with
relative ease. Fill each shell with a scoop of French Vanilla Ice Cream (p. 10)
and drizzle with Melba Sauce (p. 68) or Strawberry Coulis (p. 73).
If desired, top with a swirl of whipped cream.*

1 recipe Italian Meringue (p. 80)

Preheat the oven to 200°F. Line 2 baking sheets with parchment paper. Anchor the parchment to the baking sheets by putting a small dab of Italian Meringue under each corner. Using a pencil, trace four 3-inch circles onto each sheet of parchment.

Using a rubber spatula, spread a $^1/_2$-inch-thick disk of meringue inside each circle to make the bottom of the shells. Fill a large pastry bag fitted with a $^1/_2$- to $^3/_4$-inch plain tip with the remaining meringue. Pipe 2 to 3 rings around the outside edge of each round to form the sides of the shells.

Bake the meringues for about 2 hours, or until they are dry and crisp, but not at all brown. Remove the baking sheets from the oven and set on wire racks to cool completely. Peel the meringue shells from the parchment paper. Store the thoroughly cooled meringue shells in an airtight container at room temperature for up to 1 week. **Makes 8 shells.**

*Meringue Boats:* Line 2 baking sheets with parchment paper. Using a pencil, trace three 3-by-6-inch ovals, or boat shapes, onto each sheet of parchment. Proceed as directed with the recipe. **Makes 6 boats.**

# Ice Cream Truffles

*Like the chocolate candies, these sweet confections made from ice cream are called truffles because they visually resemble the rare and famous subterranean delicacy of that name. Any flavor ice cream will work well.*

24 chocolate wafers
2 tablespoons instant coffee
   powder (optional)

2½ to 3 cups French Vanilla Ice
   Cream (p. 10) or
   Chocolate Ice Cream (p. 12)

Chill a jelly-roll pan or shallow baking pan. In a food processor fitted with the metal blade, process the chocolate wafers until finely ground. Or, using a rolling pin, crush the wafers between 2 pieces of waxed paper to make fine crumbs. Place the crumbs and coffee, if desired, in a shallow dish.

Using a small scoop or a measuring tablespoon, scoop walnut-sized balls of the ice cream and place them on the chilled pan; if necessary, freeze until firm.

Insert a wooden skewer into an ice cream ball and roll it in the crumb mixture to coat. Return the "truffle" to the pan and remove the skewer. Repeat with the remaining ice cream balls. Freeze the truffles until firm. Serve in foil bonbon cups, if desired. **Makes 28 truffles.**

*Ice Cream-Walnut Truffles:* In a food processor fitted with the metal blade, process 2 cups walnuts until finely ground. Coat the ice cream balls in the nuts and freeze until firm.

# Banana Splits

*Serving a banana split in a meringue "boat" gives the old ice cream parlor favorite a new look, and we also like the idea of edible containers. For a children's party, further pursue the nautical theme by using drinking straws and scraps of colorful fabric to rig up tiny sails. If time is short, use store-bought ice cream.*

6 Meringue Boats (p. 81)

1 pint Chocolate Ice Cream
(p. 12)

1 pint Philadelphia Strawberry
Ice Cream (p. 24)

1 pint French Vanilla Ice Cream
(p. 10)

3 large ripe but unblemished
bananas

1 recipe Mocha Sauce (p. 72),
warmed

Whipped cream, for decoration
(optional)

½ cup coarsely chopped nuts,
lightly toasted, for decoration
(optional)

Fresh strawberries, for
decoration (optional)

Make the meringue "boats" and the ice creams according to their recipes.

Peel the bananas and cut in half. Slice each half lengthwise into quarters. Arrange 4 pieces of banana around the sides of each meringue boat.

Place 1 scoop of each ice cream into each boat. Spoon the warm Mocha Sauce over and around the ice cream. Decorate with whipped cream, nuts, and fresh strawberries, if desired. **Serves 6.**

# Mocha Ice Cream Sandwiches

*Ever since the Earl of Sandwich discovered that he could
eat roast beef without leaving the gambling tables if he placed it between
two slices of bread, the idea of the sandwich has attained enormous
popularity. It is not surprising that the concept would eventually be translated
even to ice cream. This recipe and the variation suggested may appeal
to the adult palate more than to children, but plain vanilla, chocolate,
or chocolate chip ice cream can be substituted for a kids' version.*

½ cup unsalted butter, softened

1 cup sugar

1 large egg

2 ounces unsweetened chocolate, melted and slightly cooled

1 teaspoon pure vanilla extract

1½ cups all-purpose flour

¼ teaspoon cream of tartar

¼ teaspoon salt

1 quart Mocha Chunk Ice Cream (p. 18) or Cappuccino Ice Cream (p. 13), slightly softened

In a large bowl, using an electric mixer set at medium-high, cream together the butter and sugar until light and fluffy. Beat in the egg, melted chocolate, and vanilla until well blended.

In a small bowl, combine the flour, cream of tartar, and salt. Reduce the mixer speed to low and beat in the flour mixture until well blended.

Gather the dough into a ball, wrap in plastic; chill for at least 1 hour or freeze for about 20 minutes, until firm.

Preheat the oven to 400°F. Divide the dough in half. Return half to the refrigerator while you work with the other half. On a piece of parchment or waxed paper, roll out the dough to a ¼-inch thickness. Using a 3-inch round cookie or biscuit cutter, cut out cookies. Gather the scraps and roll them out, and cut out more cookies. Carefully transfer the cookies to an ungreased baking

sheet, spacing them about 1 inch apart.

Bake the cookies for about 8 minutes, or until the edges begin to crisp. Set the baking sheet on a wire rack to cool for 5 minutes. Transfer the cookies to the rack to cool completely. Repeat as directed with the remaining dough.

To assemble the sandwiches, using a small metal spatula, spread the ice cream onto half of the cookies. Place the remaining cookies on top and gently press together. Place the sandwiches on a chilled baking sheet and freeze until ready to serve. **Makes 12 sandwiches.**

*Spiced Peach Ice Cream Sandwiches:* Prepare the cookies as directed, omitting the chocolate and adding ¾ teaspoon cinnamon, ½ teaspoon ground ginger, and ¼ teaspoon ground allspice. Fill the cookies with Philadelphia Peach Ice Cream, p. 23.

# Tropical Fruit Frappé

*The French word* frappé *means "chilled or iced" and usually refers to a slushy, frozen drink made with a sugar syrup, sometimes flavored with liqueur. In some regions of the United States, milk shakes are called frappés.*

1 cup water
¾ cup sugar
3 to 4 thin strips lime zest
One 3-inch cinnamon stick
1 medium-size ripe mango

1 large ripe banana
¼ cup fresh lime juice
Slices of lime and ripe carambola (star fruit) or small wedges of fresh pineapple or papaya, for decoration (optional)

In a medium saucepan, combine the water, sugar, lime zest, and cinnamon stick. Bring the mixture to a boil over medium heat, stirring occasionally, until the sugar is dissolved. Then boil the syrup for 3 to 4 minutes without stirring. Remove the pan from the heat. Strain the syrup through a fine sieve set over a medium bowl. Freeze the mixture for 30 minutes.

Peel and slice the mango and banana. In a food processor fitted with the metal blade or a blender, combine the mango, banana, lime juice, and chilled syrup. Process or blend until the mixture is pureed. Transfer the mixture to a medium bowl or container and freeze for 1 hour, or until firm.

To serve, put the frozen mixture in a food processor fitted with the metal blade or a blender and process until just slushy. Pour the frappé into tall chilled glasses. Decorate with fresh fruit, if desired. Serve immediately. **Serves 2.**

# Ice Cream Sodas

*To make professional-looking ice cream sodas at home,*
*use soda water from a rechargeable siphon bottle, and serve in tall glasses*
*with long-handled ice tea spoons for stirring and colorful straws for sipping.*

## Raspberry Ice Cream Soda

*picture opposite*

3 tablespoons Melba Sauce
   (p. 68)

I cup soda water or seltzer, chilled

I to 2 scoops Philadelphia
   Raspberry Ice Cream
   (variation, p. 24)

Whipped cream, for decoration
   (optional)

Fresh mint leaves, for
   decoration (optional)

Pour the sauce into a tall chilled glass. Add ¼ cup of the soda water and stir until well blended. Place the ice cream in the glass and add enough of the remaining soda water to fill the glass. Stir gently, and top with whipped cream and mint leaves, if desired. **Serves 1.**

## Chocolate Ice Cream Soda

2 to 3 tablespoons chocolate syrup

I cup soda water or seltzer, chilled

I to 2 scoops French Vanilla Ice
   Cream (p. 10)

Whipped cream, for decoration
   (optional)

Chocolate shavings, for
   decoration (p. 12; optional)

Pour the syrup into a tall chilled glass. Add ¼ cup of the soda water and stir until well blended. Place the ice cream in the glass and add enough of the remaining water to fill the glass. Stir gently, and top with whipped cream and chocolate shavings, if desired. **Serves 1.**

# Milk Shakes

*The standard recipe for this soda fountain classic
is to combine cold milk with vanilla extract or flavored syrup and
1 or 2 scoops of ice cream, blend quickly, and serve in a tall frosty glass.
Here are two versions, one using banana and the other a favorite
Mexican flavor combination of chocolate and cinnamon.*

## Top Banana Shake

1 cup milk, chilled

1 to 2 scoops Banana Ice Cream
(p. 35)

1 tablespoon rum (optional)

1½ teaspoons pure vanilla extract

Whipped cream, for decoration
(optional)

Freshly grated nutmeg,
for decoration (optional)

In a blender, combine the milk, ice cream, rum if desired, and vanilla and blend until smooth. Pour the shake into a tall chilled glass. Top with whipped cream and sprinkle with nutmeg, if desired. **Serves 1.**

## Mexican Malted Shake

1 cup milk, chilled

3 tablespoons chocolate syrup

1 tablespoon powdered malted milk

1 to 2 scoops Chocolate Ice Cream (p. 12)
or Cappuccino Ice Cream (p.13)

¼ teaspoon cinnamon

Whipped cream, for decoration
(optional)

Cinnamon, for decoration (optional)

In a blender, combine the milk, syrup, malted milk, ice cream, and cinnamon and blend until smooth. Pour into a tall frosted glass. Top with whipped cream and cinnamon, if desired. **Serves 1.**

To make ice cream or sorbet without an ice cream machine, pour the custard or sorbet mixture into a stainless steel bowl and place it in the freezer. When the mixture begins to firm, beat using an electric mixer set at medium-high or whisk until light and fluffy, then return it to the freezer. Repeat this process 2 or 3 times, or until the frozen mixture has a light, less icy texture.

If you are making custard-based ice cream, after beating the custard for the last time, fold in the whipped cream and other ingredients, such as nuts or chocolate chips, that are called for in the recipe. Complete the freezing process. To give sorbets volume and a fluffy texture, gently fold 1 to 2 cups of Italian Meringue (p. 80) into the mixture after the final beating, then return it to the freezer until firm. This method will never produce quite the texture and volume achieved with an ice cream maker, but the results are good.

If you prefer using an ice cream maker, there are several kinds on the market to choose from. Crank machines, both manually operated or electric, consist of a bucket, usually made of slatted wood, containing a metal canister inside with a removable lid. A paddle or dasher rotates inside the canister when an external

handle, or crank, is turned. The ice cream or sorbet is chilled by a mixture of cracked ice and rock salt that is layered and firmly packed inside the wooden bucket around the canister. These machines are a bit messy to use but can produce excellent ice cream.

Many machines require neither rock salt nor ice. The simplest model is placed directly in the freezer. An electric cord is run out of the freezer to a nearby outlet; a motor churns the ice cream and a small fan circulates cold air around the canister.

The prechilled canister or Donvier-type freezer features a metal canister containing a sealed coolant, which is placed in the freezer for 8 hours or overnight. The frozen canister is placed in a larger container and a dasher is inserted. The ice cream mixture is poured in; a lid is then attached and a crank is inserted. The crank is turned every 2 to 3 minutes until the mixture is frozen. These machines produce fair results.

The ultimate ice cream machine is the self-contained electric freezer. Freezing coils are wrapped around the canister and the dasher churns the ice cream as it freezes. These freestanding machines are expensive, but yield excellent results with ease.

**Texture:** The most desirable texture for a custard-based ice cream is entirely a matter of personal preference. For a dense, rich texture, add heavy cream to the chilled custard before freezing in an ice cream machine. A lighter, fluffier texture can be obtained by whipping the heavy cream called for in the recipe and gently folding it into the custard mixture halfway through the freezing process. If chopped fruit, nuts, or chocolate chips are included in the recipe, they should be added at this time.

**Developing time:** Ice creams and sorbets may be eaten as soon as they are frozen, but custard- and cream-based ice creams improve in flavor and texture if stored in the freezer for at least 1 hour before serving.

**Storage:** Ice creams and sorbets should be tightly packed in airtight containers and stored in the freezer; between 0° and 10° F is ideal. (If left uncovered, they develop an icy texture and pick up freezer odors.) For the best texture, ice cream should not be kept frozen for more than 3 days. Sorbets are best served immediately after freezing.

**Baked Alaska:** A dessert in which solidly frozen ice cream is placed on a layer of sponge cake and frosted with meringue; the cake is placed in a hot oven or under the broiler to brown lightly. It is sometimes called Omelet Surprise.

**Black cow:** An ice cream soda made with vanilla ice cream and cola.

**Bombe:** A frozen dessert made by lining a spherical mold with ice cream or sorbet. The center cavity is then filled with a mousse, cream, or parfait mixture. The mold is tightly sealed and the dessert is frozen solid before unmolding and serving.

**Brown cow:** An ice cream soda made with vanilla ice cream and root beer.

**Coupe:** Ice cream that is topped with fruit and served in stemmed glass or silver goblets.

**Custard-based ice cream:** Ice cream made with a cooked custard base to which flavorings and heavy cream are added.

**Frappe:** The term (from the French word *frappé*) describes a simple sugar syrup mixed with fruit or other flavorings and frozen, then processed to a slushy consistency. It can be served as a drink or dessert. In some regions of the United States, a milk shake is called a frappe.

**Frosted:** A soda fountain term used to describe a milk shake in which the ice cream is soft enough that the beverage can be consumed without a spoon.

**Frozen Yogurt:** A mixture of yogurt, sweetener, and flavorings such as fruit puree, frozen in an ice cream machine. It has the consistency of soft ice cream.

**Gaufrette:** A delicate wafer cookie, honeycombed and fan-shaped, made on an oblong iron and typically served with ice cream.

**Gelato:** An Italian ice cream made with a base of milk or egg yolks and milk. Usually denser and more icy in texture than American ice cream, it is also often more strongly flavored.

**Granita:** A mixture of water, sugar, and liquid flavorings such as fruit juice or coffee that is stirred occasionally while being frozen to create a granular texture.

**Ice cream soda:** A beverage made of carbonated water, a flavored syrup, and a scoop or two of ice cream.

**Ice milk:** A sorbet to which a small amount of milk has been added. It has a lighter, icier texture than ice cream because of its lower butterfat content.

**Malted milk:** A milk shake to which malted milk powder, a preparation of pure cow's milk and extracts of malted barley and wheat, is added.

**Melba:** A sauce made from raspberries, sugar, and lemon juice. Peach Melba is a dessert of poached peach halves, vanilla ice cream, and Melba sauce.

**Milk shake:** Milk, ice cream, and a syrup or other flavorings mixed in a blender until the ice cream is softened enough to be sipped through a straw.

**Mousse:** A frozen dessert consisting of either a flavored custard or a fruit puree lightened with whipped cream.

**Parfait:** A dessert consisting of ice cream layered with a dessert sauce, fruit, or liqueur. In France, a parfait is a frozen dessert containing either whipped cream and Italian meringue or just whipped cream. Both desserts are served in tall narrow footed glasses.

**Philadelphia ice cream:** An ice cream made without eggs, using various combinations of milk, cream, sugar, and flavorings such as fruit. Its texture is grainier than custard-based ice cream. Also called uncooked ice cream.

**Pizzelles:** Thin decoratively patterned Italian wafer cookies that are made in an iron similar to a waffle iron. They may be flat or rolled into ice cream cones.

**Rock salt:** A crystalline form of salt that is mixed with cracked ice to freeze ice cream.

**Sherbet:** A smooth frozen ice flavored with fruit and sugar, or with a mixture of fruit, sugar, and milk or cream.

**Simple syrup:** A mixture of sugar and water that is simmered until the sugar is dissolved, then sometimes boiled for 1 to 2 minutes. Also called sugar syrup, it can be used as a base for sorbets and as a foundation for candies.

**Sorbet:** A smooth frozen ice made with flavored liquids, either sweet or savory. It is different from sherbet in that it never contains dairy products.

**Spoom:** A fruit- or wine-based ice to which Italian meringue is added when the ice is halfway frozen. Spooms are traditionally served in stemmed glasses.

**Sundae:** A dessert of ice cream served with one or more toppings, such as flavored syrup, dessert sauce, whipped cream, nuts, etc. It is said to have originated in the state of Massachusetts when a law prohibiting the sale of all soft beverages on Sunday was passed. An enterprising soda jerk combined the ingredients of an ice cream soda but omitted the carbonated beverage to create the first "sundae."

## WEIGHTS

| OUNCES AND POUNDS | METRICS |
|---|---|
| ¼ ounce | 7 grams |
| ⅓ ounce | 10 grams |
| ½ ounce | 14 grams |
| 1 ounce | 28 grams |
| 1½ ounces | 42 grams |
| 1¾ ounces | 50 grams |
| 2 ounces | 57 grams |
| 3 ounces | 85 grams |
| 3½ ounces | 100 grams |
| 4 ounces (¼ pound) | 114 grams |
| 6 ounces | 170 grams |
| 8 ounces (½ pound) | 227 grams |
| 9 ounces | 250 grams |
| 16 ounces (1 pound) | 464 grams |

## LIQUID MEASURES

tsp.: teaspoon
Tbs.: tablespoon

| SPOONS AND CUPS | METRIC EQUIVALENTS |
|---|---|
| ¼ tsp. | 1.23 milliliters |
| ½ tsp. | 2.5 milliliters |
| ¾ tsp. | 3.7 milliliters |
| 1 tsp. | 5 milliliters |
| 1 dessertspoon | 10 milliliters |
| 1 Tbs. (3 tsp.) | 15 milliliters |
| 2 Tbs. (1 ounce) | 30 milliliters |
| ¼ cup | 60 milliliters |
| ⅓ cup | 80 milliliters |
| ½ cup | 120 milliliters |
| ⅔ cup | 160 milliliters |
| ¾ cup | 180 milliliters |
| 1 cup (8 ounces) | 240 milliliters |
| 2 cups (1 pint) | 480 milliliters |
| 3 cups | 720 milliliters |
| 4 cups (1 quart) | 1 litre |
| 4 quarts (1 gallon) | 3¾ litres |

## TEMPERATURES

| °F (FAHRENHEIT) | °C (CENTIGRADE OR CELSIUS) |
|---|---|
| 32 (water freezes) | 0 |
| 200 | 95 |
| 212 (water boils) | 100 |
| 250 | 120 |
| 275 | 135 |
| 300 (slow oven) | 150 |
| 325 | 160 |
| 350 (moderate oven) | 175 |
| 375 | 190 |
| 400 (hot oven) | 205 |
| 425 | 220 |
| 450 (very hot oven) | 232 |
| 475 | 245 |
| 500 (extremely hot oven) | 260 |

## LENGTH

| U.S. MEASUREMENTS | METRIC EQUIVALENTS |
|---|---|
| ⅛ inch | 3mm |
| ¼ inch | 6mm |
| ⅜ inch | 1 cm |
| ½ inch | 1.2 cm |
| ¾ inch | 2 cm |
| 1 inch | 2.5 cm |
| 1¼ inches | 3.1 cm |
| 1½ inches | 3.7 cm |
| 2 inches | 5 cm |
| 3 inches | 7.5 cm |
| 4 inches | 10 cm |
| 5 inches | 12.5 cm |

## APPROXIMATE EQUIVALENTS

1 kilo is slightly more than 2 pounds
1 litre is slightly more than 1 quart
1 meter is slightly over 3 feet
1 centimeter is approximately ⅜ inch

# INDEX